RISE
ABOVE YOURSELF

Rise Above Yourself

A guide to self growth

JULIA COROTAN

Amica Mea by Julia

CONTENTS

Dedication   viii

I	Preface	1
II	Fear	5
III	Exercise 1	10
IV	Weaknesses	12
V	Exercise 2	19
VI	Strengths	21
VII	Exercise 3	26
VIII	Becoming the person, you want to be	28

IX   Exercise 4   32

About The Author   34

Copyright © 2021 by Julia Corotan

All rights reserved. No part of this book may be reproduced in any manner whatsoever without written permission except in the case of brief quotations embodied in critical articles and reviews.

First Printing, 2021

This guide is dedicated to AIESEC. To the people who stood by me, became life long friends and family. Thank you. This one is for you

Preface

As a child, I was always shy. Yet, I was always so fascinated with studying my surroundings. I love to read, to know more about the world around me, to soak up as much random knowledge as I can. But I was always so terrified to go out and explore. Growing up, I was always comfortable being alone, observing what was happening around me. I just wanted to be that person in the background who kept to herself.

When I was in high school, I was still a shy kid. I wanted to step out of my comfort zone, but I was always so terrified to do so. When I discovered sports, I joined the girls' softball varsity team, where I became the pitcher for the team. Standing on that field on that pitcher's mound in the center of the Softball Diamond,[1] I would feel the surge of adrenaline. The feeling of being invincible and forgetting ever being that shy kid. It was just me, the ball, and the batter. However, there were still many countless losses with all the wins, especially during games where

I didn't play my best. Times where my coach had to pull me out of the game to get my mind back together, those instances terrified me since I felt that I had let my coach and my team down.

In university, this was where I finally got the taste of what it would feel like to step out of my comfort zone. I had moved away at the young age of eighteen to the country my parents were born and raised in, The Philippines. I had to live there without my parents. I needed to learn to be independent to survive. It was in university where I was constantly pushed to step out of my comfort zone, face my fears, understand my weaknesses, and use my strengths to my advantage.

When I think of my fears and my weaknesses, I get propelled back to high school. To all those times where I had to sit out of a game to clear my head so that I could go back and play the next inning.[2] Once I could get my mind cleared, I would be able to focus more on the game and to know what I did wrong and not let my opponents use my weaknesses against me. It was just me, the ball, and the batter.

That's how I look at life today. When I need to present on stage in front of many, or when I need to present my product, it's just me and my presentation. Life is full of countless failures and people taking advantage of your fears and weaknesses. But it's through those that we learn to pick ourselves up and do better.

Today, at this moment, if you ask me to step out of my comfort zone to not be shy, I would gladly do it. I had found that the best opportunities lie outside our comfort zones; countless opportunities that we always thought were unreachable are actually within our reach. We just have to put a foot out the door. I had been pushed and driven out of my comfort zone so many times since my university days. I had been taught to identify my strength, weaknesses, and fears. To be able to use those to my advantage. To understand them and not let them control me. To overcome my fears and weaknesses, understand myself, become a better individual, and finally Rise Above Myself.

So, when the idea was brought up, to write a guidebook about overcoming fears and weaknesses and using our strengths to our advantage. I thought of the very first time I ever presented this particular topic. It was back in October of 2019 at a conference I helped facilitate for three colleges in the Philippines.

I spoke on improving oneself by identifying your fears and weaknesses and by using your strengths to your advantage. I've presented this topic numerous times after that, once in the United Kingdom and the other in Malawi. This topic has come a long way, but it has helped many youths and young individuals along the way. So, I thought, why not create a short guidebook to share with those who weren't able to attend the conferences, workshops, and seminars I've spoken about this topic in. And that is how this guidebook was born. It has improved a lot along the way, and it has had many more experiences added to it, but the essence still remains the same.

I hope this guidebook helps you just as much as it has helped the many individuals before you.

"Rise above yourself."

1. A softball or baseball field is shaped like a diamond
2. A softball term for a round per game. There are seven innings per game

| ii |

Fear

Why is it important to identify our strengths, weakness, and fears? As humans, we tend to not like exploring our weaknesses and fears and only focusing on our strengths and how to use them. I use to think like that. As much as possible, I wanted to stay away from anything that made me vulnerable. However, over the years, I have realized that it is crucial to identify our weaknesses and fears and not just focus on our strengths. It is called balance.

Identifying our fears and weaknesses will help us know and better understand the areas that we need to improve on. No human is perfect; we are all imperfect. There are many areas of our lives that we need to understand to improve ourselves. We are a constant work in progress. Identifying our fears and our weak spots gives us a better, more precise understanding of ourselves. I never understood when people would tell me, *"I know you better than you know yourself."* I would always question this. How could someone know me more than I know myself? But over the years, I have seen that particular statement come to life. I would watch friends or family constantly improve their work and their understanding of themselves, and I wondered how they were able to do that.

"No human is perfect; we are all imperfect."

It was not until a particular conversation with a friend that I realized how important it was to identify our areas of improvement and not shy away from them. Identifying those areas gives us an advantage in life and a better understanding of ourselves.

So before we begin and deep dive into ways, we can understand our fears, weaknesses, and strengths. Let us first clearly define them. Firstly, according to the Miriam-Webster Dictionary, ***fear is an unpleasant, often strong emotion caused by anticipation or awareness of danger***. So, yes, fear is an emotion. It is an emotion that we are all aware of and can at least identify one instance in our life when we exhibited fear.

We, as humans, try as much as possible to stay away from anything that scares us. If we can ignore those emotions for the rest of our lives, I am sure we would. However, there is nothing wrong with fear or experiencing fear. It is better to identify what terrifies us because, in all honesty, and I really mean all honesty, we can use those fears to our advantage.

> **"We, as humans, try as much as possible to stay away from anything that scares us."**

So let me put it this way. I mentioned earlier that when I was in university, I was constantly put in situations that made me uncomfortable. Which tested my every being—many of those situations that I was placed in tested my fears. One major fear of mine is failure. I was never particularly good in school; I was just an average student. I never stood out academically. So you might wonder why failure terrifies me. Well, let me tell you, I, however, did stand out in sports and other extracurricular activities. In those areas, I was scared to fail because it was something I was good at, it was where I excelled, and it was an outlet that I could constantly work on to improve my skills. Back in university, I joined a Nonprofit organization called AIESEC.

AIESEC is a youth leadership organization that is present in over one hundred countries. While working in AIESEC, so many of my skills were tested, it was also through this organization that I was able to grow and better understand myself. I mentioned failure and how terrified I am of failure. Especially failing in something that I am either good at or something that I love to do and have poured out my heart and soul.

When I joined AIESEC, I was given an opportunity to become the Vice President for Marketing and Communications for one of the local branches of AIESEC in the Philippines. I had a chance to mentor and coach eleven individuals who were part of that department. The local branch I was part of was not as big as the other branches around the Philippines.

"The best lesson in life is failure."

The chapter I worked for had roughly around thirty-two members. My department was one of the biggest departments in that branch.[3] I had one year to mentor and coach my members; however, I was terrified since I had only joined AIESEC a few months back, and I was still learning about the organization. I was scared that I would not be the leader that my members needed me to be. I always thought I would let them down, and I would fail as a leader, and my fears got the best of me.

I do, however, admit that I had let my members down. I wasn't the best leader at that time. I was still learning about myself about the organization and how to lead eleven individuals to become better versions of themselves.

I admitted to my fear, and I admitted to my failure. I acknowledged that I was scared and let it overpower me instead of trying to learn to be better through it. When I noticed that I had failed my members by not being the leader they expected me to be and not being the mentor, they thought I would be. I focused on learning from my mistakes, looking at the areas I went wrong on, and trying my best to improve. Although it was too late when I realized my mistakes, I was given another opportunity to lead them. This time, however, I had much more responsibilities, more members that looked up to me and expected me to lead them to teach them what AIESEC is about and why we do what we do in AIESEC, which was to develop future leaders.

I was voted in to be President for that local branch for the term 2019-2020. I was happy that I was given another opportunity to learn, grow, and be a better leader and a better individual. However, my fear of failure still remained. I was still scared that I would let my members down because this time, I did not just have eleven people that would look up to me. I had over forty people who trusted me to lead the entity and lead them and my team and to represent our branch in both National and International plenaries.

When I saw that it was time to fully step out of my comfort zone, I used my fear to my advantage. To learn from the experiences of my previous position to be the leader my members expected me to be but to also be the person I wanted to be. I could not do that if I had my fear stop me. It was time to step out of that comfort zone, and it was time to conquer that fear. ***Because the best lesson in life is failure***.

---

3. In AIESEC, once you are part of the executive board, your term would run for one year, and you could get re-elected again if you decide to run for a position for the following period.

| iii |

Exercise 1

What can you do to overcome your fear? to be able to step out of your comfort zone? to become a better leader, a better individual and start growing not for others but for yourself.

I want you to ask yourself the following questions: Write your answers down if you want to so you can come back later on to look back at what you wanted to overcome.

Question 1: What am I afraid of?

Question 2: What are the outcomes and what do I accomplish when I overpower my fears?

Question 3: What can I do to work on my fears to not let them scare me?

Question 4: Are you scared of failure? Why?

| iv |

Weaknesses

Someone once told me that for us to become stronger, we must first face our weaknesses. I used to dislike that saying because, just like everyone, why would I want to meet my weakness. Why could I not just push them to the farthest corners of my mind and leave them there? I did not want to come face to face with anything that would hinder me from achieving my goals. But that is precisely it. If we do not face our weakness, it will just keep pulling us back and maybe even stop us from achieving and going beyond what we want to accomplish in life.

So, as much as we dislike it or even hate it. We have to come face to face with our weaknesses. We need to identify those weaknesses and see what areas we could improve. But we also have to understand that we would not improve on all those areas overnight. Our weaknesses are a work in progress. Some are easier to improve in than others.

Before we begin identifying ways to help improve our weaknesses, let us define what weakness actually means in this context. According to the Cambridge Dictionary, *"weakness can be defined as a particular part or quality of someone or something that is not good or effective."* So let us look at weaknesses this way. Think of yourself as a product; every product, when created, has a weakness. No product is perfect once it comes out of production. That is why it goes through many trials before it gets put out on the market. The people behind the production of the product would look at the many different areas that the product would need to be improved on. Once the product gets put out on the market, it is not entirely perfect. It would look perfect; however, there would still be many areas of improvement. But the company would only see those areas once the product has been used and tested by the people who buy those products.

Remember I said to view yourself as a product? Well, now let us talk about that. Every human is technically a product of its own kind. Once we are born, we are not perfect. There will be many areas that we would need to grow and improve on. We go through school to strengthen those areas and learn about ourselves and what we can do, and what we are good at. That is what school is for. School is seen as the trial period. Once we graduate from school, we are placed out in the market where we start looking for jobs, start earning money and starting to test the skills we had learned and developed while in school. Once we get to experience the real world, that is when we would be able to see the many areas we would need to improve on. Those areas are what we call our weaknesses.

Often times we do not want to acknowledge those weaknesses because we think those weaknesses are not too significant to affect our everyday lives. That is where we are actually wrong. Those minor weaknesses that we see in ourselves can stop us or even pull us back from our true potential. Just like an actual product, there are many weaknesses to it. Some may be seen as minor problems, but those problems tend to be ignored compared to the major ones because companies do not know the importance or significance of its improvement yet. Once other companies with similar products start improving those minor problems, it is only noticed that there is a need to turn their products into a much better version.

> **"Those little weaknesses that we see in ourselves can actually stop us or even pull us back from our true potential."**

We don't see the need for improvements as humans until we see others succeeding and becoming better than they were before. That is why there is competition because we tend to want to be better than others, but we do not know what or how to improve just yet.

But ask yourself this why do we need to compete with others when we can just compete with ourselves? Can't we see our past selves as competition? When you look at yourself now, do you want to be a better version of yourself in the future? Or are you satisfied with how you are now? Maybe you are, and you don't see the need to improve. But why don't you challenge yourself? See what it is like when you identify those areas of weakness. It could be small, or it could be immense. Identify them and see your improvements and accomplishments in a few months. And get back to me about that.

Once upon a time I use to not see the need to improve myself. I was once just satisfied with how life was. I had everything planned out, and all I had to do was follow that plan, and all will be good. It was not until I saw the improvements of the people around me and the results when I would constantly challenge myself and step out of my comfort zone and it really got me thinking. What are ways I could improve myself? No one is perfect, so I am sure I have flaws that need to be improved. What are areas of myself that I can assess and see if I can work through them. Then compare the results in a few months.

"No one is perfect."

I was in AIESEC when I saw the need to improve myself. In AIESEC, we were always given many opportunities to constantly challenge ourselves if we take advantage of those opportunities. One of those opportunities was to be part of the executive board. As I mentioned in "Part 1: Fear." You now know I was part of the executive board twice, first when I was Vice President for Marketing and Communications and Second when I was President.

However, I actually held four significant positions in AIESEC; the first two were mentioned earlier. The last two positions were after my term as President. I applied for and was accepted as a Social Media Manager for AIESEC in the United Kingdom for the National team.[4] Lastly, I became National Digital Marketing and Communications Director for AIESEC in Malawi.[5] Throughout all those positions, I was given a chance to improve the areas I needed to improve on.

I have many weaknesses that I still work on. I say still because I may have slightly improved on some, but I have not entirely improved on all. The following are what I consider my weaknesses, **time management, procrastination, and public speaking.** You might look at those and think, how are they my weaknesses given my current career of being a blogger and a CEO of a mentoring and coaching company. So let me explain why; time management was never my strong suit; that is why I also wrote procrastinate down as a weakness as well. I was never good at balancing my time or doing tasks ahead of time. I always like to put doing anything to the last minute.

When I was studying for my undergraduate, I had many assignments and tasks that I needed to start days in advance to complete. Still, I could never begin them ahead of time. When I became part of AIESEC, especially when I was part of the executive board, we had many deliverables that needed to be done ahead of time. That was when I realized I needed to balance my time to be able to manage and get everything done by the due date. I learned that I could set aside at least an hour or two of my day to work on any critical tasks that needed to be completed.

I've gotten slightly better at it. I can put aside a few hours in my day to work. However, I still have days where I leave everything all to the last minute. That is why it is still a work in progress. I have seen the improvements, but I am still nowhere near being perfect.

Public speaking, if you ask anyone I have worked with or are close friends with, they will tell you I am terrified of speaking in front of large crowds. However, if you look at my resume and the positions I've held, you wonder why I would be so terrified of public speaking. Even though I have done probably done hundreds of public speaking engagements, facilitated many conferences and workshops, talked in front of huge crowds, and even took part in many businesses' proposal defenses in front of countless panels. Public speaking is still something I am working on.

I mentioned that I was a shy kid, and I still consider myself shy even though I like to step out of my comfort zone. I'm still a timid individual. That is why talking in front of people scares me. But over the years, I have learned to not let it overpower me. I have found ways to combat that fear to actually let me enjoy talking in front of crowds. Yes, I still get scared, especially before any speaking engagements that I have to take part in. But once I'm out there, once I get to do what I love, my fears slowly creep away.

All my weaknesses are still a work in progress. Even though I have gotten better at talking in front of crowds and balancing my time, Julia, in her early 20's would be proud. I am still, however, trying to improve and to be better. I am a work in progress, just like everyone. I may seem confident on the outside, but I still have weaknesses that I need to work on.

"I am a work in progress just like everyone."

4. This was the team that oversaw all local AIESEC branches

5. The Malawi branch of AIESEC

| v |

Exercise 2

So, what can you do to identify your weaknesses? to be able to work through them and find ways to improve? To be a better individual to be able to challenge yourself more.

Ask yourself the following questions. Write your answers down if you want to so you can come back later on to look back at what you wanted to overcome.

Question 1: What do I consider my weaknesses?

Question 2: What areas of my life do I still need to improve on?

Questions 3: What can I do to challenge myself and overcome my weaknesses?

Question 4: What can I do to combat those fears?

| vi |

Strengths

When people ask about your strengths, what comes to mind? Is it what you are good at? is it what people think you are good at? or is it what you have already improved on and what you now consider something you are good at? In truth, it is all the above questions I have mentioned. It can be more, but the essence of our strengths is what I had mentioned above.

So let us define strengths. According to the Cambridge dictionary, strength can be defined as ***"The ability to do things that need a lot of physical or mental effort."*** You might ask, is being good at photography a strength? or is being a good communicator considered a strength? The answer to all those questions is yes; they are all considered strengths. Because they take a lot of physical and mental effort to produce good results.

So let me give you an example. Let me tell you about my strengths and what I consider areas that I am good at or what the people who have worked closely with me have told me I am good at. Before I started working for AIESEC, I already had areas that I had considered strengths. Some I have already identified in high school; some were when I started university. So, what are my strengths? This is not everything, but this is what I consider essential, **communication, empathy, creativity, positivity, and leadership.**

Over the years and throughout my career, I have always used my strengths to my advantage. I would not, however, consider them perfect. Yes, they are areas that I am particularly good at and that have made me stand out in different roles and jobs that I have done over the years. However, don't get me wrong, even though they are already considered my strengths, there are still many areas that I could improve on.

> **"Life is full of learning. What makes it great is learning that we can improve and build on areas that we are already skilled in."**

In AIESEC, I got to use and improve on all my strengths. Through AIESEC, I realized and learned that our strengths do not just end when we think we are already good at them. No, the learning process continues. Just like our weaknesses and fears, these are also areas that we can constantly improve. To be better.

Let's go back to the product analogy that I had talked about in "Part 2: Weaknesses." Look at all the products that have been released for the public to buy and use—for example, a mobile phone. We now have mobile phones because of the convenience they give us nowadays. I want you to think back to 40 years ago when mobile phones did not exist. However, there was the telephone that can be used to communicate with others. It was faster than writing and sending letters but not as convenient as mobile phones today.

Today we can bring our phones everywhere. We can call from wherever we are, message whoever we want, and also have the ability to access the internet without having to constantly carry our laptops around. When telephones were created, it was an improvement from writing and communicating through letters with the advancement of technology. Telephones still had to be improved even though they already had their strengths which were faster and more reliable forms of communication.

So, think of your strengths. Don't you think they have areas that require improvements? The answer should be yes. Like the telephone and our mobile phones today, there are still areas in your life that need improvement. 20 years from now, mobile phones will be very different because the people who created them will see the many areas still need of improvement. Just like you as a person 5, 10, 15 or 20 years from now you won't be the same person you are today. What you learn today will lead you to a different person tomorrow. So now let's look at our life and our strengths like that too.

"I was not a natural-born leader."

So back to my AIESEC career. If you look at my strengths, I mentioned leadership. If you remember from "Part 1: Fears," I mentioned how I was terrified I was at failing on being a good leader and mentor to my members. So, you might wonder why I would consider leadership a strength. Before AIESEC, I already had many leadership roles. I've had many leadership experiences since I was in high school. This was an area that, even though I was already good at, was an area I still wanted to improve on.

Being a leader is not an easy role. It is a role that many people look up to. Especially when you are in much higher positions, such as when I was President or the National Digital Marketing and Communications director.

I was not a natural-born leader like some. I learned to be a leader because I like to take initiative when no one else would. However, leadership is also a role that I realized I could mentor others. Teach others the skills I have learned and share my knowledge. Even though I knew what I had to do I still needed to learn how to be an effective leader. I had to learn to properly communicate problems, solutions, and tasks. Learn how important empathy is, stay positive amid crisis, and be creative to stand out. I had picked up skills in those areas over the years, but

I had to learn to use them together combine them and use them to their highest potential. In the early days I didn't yet know how to use my skills and strengths to my advantage yet and I allowed my fear of not being a successful leader over power me. Now I know that I should take advantage of my strengths and use them to its full potential.

We as people often forget that we also need to improve on our skills. Like the telephone I mentioned last time, the telephone needed to improve even though it was already successful. Just like our skills we need to constantly improve to be better; it does not mean that we are already good at it, we cannot improve any further. Life is full of learning and what makes it great is learning that we can improve and build on areas that we are already skilled in.

| vii |

Exercise 3

What do you consider your strengths? What are your skills that make you stand out from everyone else? What can you do with this skills to be a better individual to be able to challenge yourself more.

Ask yourself the following questions. Write your answers down if you want to so you can come back later on to look back at what you wanted to overcome.

Question 1: What do you consider your strengths?

Question 2: What can you do to improve on your skills?

Questions 3: What more can you do to challenge yourself to build on your already existing skills?

Question 4: What areas in your strengths do you think should be improved on?

| viii |

Becoming the person, you want to be

We are almost at the end—just a little way to go and a few more words to be said. I hope you have learned many things about yourself along the way.

Now, you have gotten this far. But are you still asking yourself why it is essential to identify your fears, weaknesses, and strengths? If yes, that's okay. It does not take overnight to learn it all. If no, congratulations! I hope you can use what you now know to your advantage. So let us start wrapping things up.

In early 2019, I was given an opportunity to attend an International Conference in Bangkok, Thailand, hosted by AIESEC Asia Pacific. The regional office of AIESEC in the Asia Pacific region. One of the sessions that I had attended was facilitated by the then Global President of AIESEC. The session was about understanding ourselves, understanding our strengths and weaknesses.

It was in that session where I saw the importance of really understanding ourselves for us to really grow as individuals and to be able to excel in our work. What I would never forget during that session was when our weaknesses weigh us down, it affects us and affects the people around us. As a former President of my local branch in AIESEC, when I am struggling, when I am weighing myself down, my performance affects me and affects my team and my members. I cannot be a leader without a team; I cannot have my entity without my members.

"Own your imperfections."

It was in that session when I saw how important it was to see, identify and understand the areas that can stop me from performing my best. My experiences are different from many, and not everyone is part of AIESEC. Not everyone has access to the same opportunities I had access to.

So let me make this easy; take a look at yourself now as a student or as a working professional and individual. What have you always wanted to work on? What areas do you want to improve but have been too scared to? and have decided to push it to the back of your mind. What parts of you are you too afraid to face? Because you think that this will stop you from discovering your true potential.

When you see others, do you often feel left out? Lost? Wanting to improve yourself but don't know how? Take all the questions and lessons that I have mentioned throughout the guide and take a look at your life now. You are bound to find the answers if you look a little deeper within yourself. I've been there. I once asked these same questions to myself not so long ago. Take a minute to just take a look. You'll be surprised by what you will find.

To end it all, let us leave ourselves with some commitments that we can give ourselves now. Commitments that can help us improve, grow and be better individuals. Promises that can help us use our fears, weaknesses, and strengths to our advantage.

These are your commitments to yourself. Take a piece of paper out or your phone, write it somewhere where you have easy access to and that you would be able to look back at, to give you a small reminder when you start to doubt yourself.

I've written out my commitments to myself that I want to share with you. The following are the promises that I've made to myself:

Constantly challenge myself
Give myself a goal
Keep track of my progress
Stop thinking about what others think of me
Always remember to take a break

So now I want you to go and write down your commitments and challenge yourself. We are all a work in progress. Even though

I know the areas I need to work on, I am still discovering many new areas that I need to improve on.

Someone once told me to Own my Imperfections. No one is perfect. It is okay to be imperfect cause knowing your imperfections will bring you to places you thought were never reachable. Owning your flaws will bring out your true potential. So, my parting words with you all are, ***"Own your imperfections."***

| ix |

Exercise 4

To wrap things up I have a few more questions that you can answer that can help you tie everything together.

Ask yourself the following questions. Write your answers down if you want to so you can come back later on to look back at what you wanted to overcome.

Question 1: What are you at your best?

Question 2: What are you at your worse?

Question 3: What peak experiences can you recall in life?

Question 4: What failing experiences can you recall in life?

Question 5: What did you learn about yourself throughout this guide?

ABOUT THE AUTHOR

Julia is a motivational and Personal Development blogger as well as the Founder and current CEO and Creative Director for MAEVC. She helps mentor and coach youths and young professionals worldwide to help prepare and equip them with skills that will align them with their professional and personal goals once they enter the workforce. She is also the Founder of the successful blog Amica Mea. Where she shares her journey, struggles, and experiences living in the Philippines. While battling with her mental health, choosing her career. And what it was like growing up as one of the few Asian children in a small town in the South Pacific country of Papua New Guinea. She is also a motivational and leadership speaker and has spoken at many conferences, seminars, and workshops hosted by AIESEC in the Philippines and numerous AIESEC branches within the Philippines, namely Miriam College, De La Salle-College of Saint

Benilde, and San Beda University as well as AIESEC in the United Kingdom and AIESEC in Malawi.

www.ingramcontent.com/pod-product-compliance
Lightning Source LLC
Chambersburg PA
CBHW071846290426
44109CB00017B/1948